WHICH WAY TO THE PROMISED LAND?
40 DAILY READINGS FOR LENT OR ANY TIME OF YEAR

WIPF & STOCK · Eugene, Oregon

Sylvia Boys

Wipf and Stock Publishers
199 W 8th Ave, Suite 3
Eugene, OR 97401

Which Way to the Promised Land
Daily Readings for Lent or Anytime
By Boys, Syliva
Copyright©2018 Apostolos
ISBN 13: 978-1-5326-6903-3
Publication date 9/16/2018
Previously published by Apostolos, 2018

Day 1: Your Way or My Way?

> *"For my thoughts are not your thoughts, neither are your ways my ways," declares the Lord. "As the heavens are higher than the earth, so are my ways higher than your ways and my thoughts than your thoughts. (Isa 55:8–9)*

Every day we are faced with the same choice. Do we choose to live life our own way or God's way? However, it is not an easy choice, and it is one we must make repeatedly. For in each new situation, we choose again, often without any conscious awareness of it. We can almost go on "autopilot" without really knowing that we have made a choice. Our choices can be good or bad, and as a result have good or bad consequences.

My way is the most natural choice for me (without Jesus). It is what feels comfortable for me and generally gives me what I want. Yet I am aware that only 2-year-olds have tantrums when they are not allowed to do what they want! They haven't yet learned that the world does not revolve around them, nor do they understand that if they always get what they want now, those choices may later have bad consequences for them or others. Sadly, from time to time we can still behave like 2-year-olds, unable to grasp that our decisions relate to a minute part of a very big picture.

Only God can see the big picture. However, the more time we choose to spend reading God's Word, and allowing it to transform us, the more able we are to see things from heaven's perspective. In Paul's letter to the Romans, chapter 12, we are encouraged to be transformed by the renewing of our minds. This involves a choice to read, meditate on, and even speak out what the Bible is saying.

John the Baptist came to encourage people to repent, because the kingdom of God is near. That is the truth. The kingdom of God is near to us, but we can only perceive it, when we have taken the time to repent (or re-think), as we compare God's Word with our thoughts and values. It is only as we read the Bible, asking the Holy Spirit to reveal to us the things which need to change in our lives, that we can see the discrepancy between our thoughts and God's thoughts, and so choose God's ways, not our ways.

Daily Reading Plan Day 1: Exodus 1–3; Psalm 31.

Day 2: Listening for God's Voice

> *The Lord said, "Go out and stand on the mountain in the presence of the Lord, for the Lord is about to pass by." Then a great and powerful wind tore the mountains apart and shattered the rocks before the Lord, but the Lord was not in the wind. After the wind there was an earthquake, but the Lord was not in the earthquake. After the earthquake came a fire, but the Lord was not in the fire. And after the fire came a gentle whisper. When Elijah heard it, he pulled his cloak over his face and went out and stood at the mouth of the cave. (1 Kings 19:11–13)*

We can only hear God's voice, and learn how to live His way, as we study His Word. We will discover more of God's character and great love for us, and be challenged to take bigger steps of faith, as we realise the great discrepancy between what we would like to do, and God's will for our lives.

Many people these days live such busy lives, that there seems no time to stop and read the Bible or pray to God. It can seem at times that we are on a treadmill, and life can feel out of control. We react to situations without considering how to respond. It is then that we do what seems natural to us, because it is quicker and easier.

It is important to take a step off the treadmill to assess and to find out what God is saying. When we understand God's perspective, we can make more informed choices. When we think that we are too busy to pray, we are in fact too busy not to pray.

We cannot keep following the same pattern of life and expect things to change. Life will only improve when we choose to do something different, following God's instruction through having insight into His Word in the Bible.

Elijah discovered that God wasn't in the wind, the earthquake, or the fire, but speaking quietly into his stilled mind. God can and does speak to us in the midst of our busy-ness, but unless we have taken the time in the quietness to get used to His voice, we will probably miss His directions when life is busy. One Word from God, and your life could be transformed. I pray that you won't miss it!

Daily Reading Plan Day 2: Exodus 4–5; Psalm 32.

Day 3: God's Plans are for Our Good

> *For we know that in all things God works for the good of those who love Him and are called according to His purpose. (Romans 8:28)*

I love this verse from Paul's letter to the Romans. God created us and He knows what is good for us. In every situation His desire is to work things out well for us. But this verse tells us that in order for things to ultimately work out well, we need to love God. However, John 14:23 tells us, *"Jesus replied, 'Anyone who loves me will obey my teaching. My Father will love them, and we will come to them and make our home with them.'"* Taken together with the verse from Romans 8, we realise that to really access God's best for our lives, we need to be obedient to Him.

Galatians 6:7 says, *"Do not be deceived: God cannot be mocked. A man reaps what he sows."* When we sow good seed in our lives, by good choices in our thoughts and actions, we eventually reap a good harvest. Sowing bad seed brings a bad harvest. The only way to be set free from a bad harvest is to repent of our wrong words and actions and ask God's forgiveness on the basis that Jesus shed His blood to pay for our sin.

If we continue to make the same bad choices, we will continue to see the same results. This is often discovered when we find ourselves saying "Oh no, not that again. That always happens to me!" We can feel like innocent victims when things seem to wrong for us, without realising that the harvest is coming from our wrong choices.

Don't give the enemy opportunity to have access to your life. Instead:

> *Be sober, be watchful. Your adversary the devil prowls around like a roaring lion, seeking someone to devour. (1 Peter 5:8)*

Even when we know in our head that we can trust God, it can take a long time before we really know this in our hearts. Sometimes we want to trust Him, but we can't quite manage it. Maybe you can relate to the verse Mark 9:24 "I do believe; help me overcome my unbelief!" God's thoughts and ways are way above our own. He can be trusted. Dare we believe Him?

Daily Reading Plan Day 3: Exodus 6–7; Psalm 33.

Day 4: Towards God or Away from God?

> *Come near to God and he will come near to you. Wash your hands, you sinners, and purify your hearts, you double-minded. (James 4:8)*

We don't succeed or fail in life by accident. Whether we are aware of it or not, the results of our lives are as a result of having made good or bad choices. Some choices take us closer to God, but others take us away from God.

But would anyone who calls himself/herself a Christian choose to move further away from God?

The problem is that unless we actively choose to move closer to God by prayer, reading the Bible, and associating with godly people, we will automatically move away from God. In addition to that, sin separates us from God. So, unless we choose to repent and receive His forgiveness, the sin will keep us from his blessings.

We need look no further than the story of Adam and Eve in the Garden of Eden, to realise that our human nature is to hide from God when we know we have done wrong. God came looking for them and asked the question "Where are you?" Of course, God knew where they were, but He was reminding them that they had moved from their usual place of meeting with God.

Not only were they hiding from God, but they had also sewn fig leaves together to hide their shame, because they realised they were naked. Before they ate the forbidden fruit, they could be totally open with God, but when they sinned they were afraid of facing God, and this enabled the enemy to step in and tell them that they should be ashamed for what they had done!

They had chosen to disobey God and did not want to be held accountable, so they hid. Is that what we do? Do we allow sin to prevent us coming to God because we know we don't deserve to be forgiven?

Daily Reading Plan Day 4: Exodus 8–9; Psalm 34.

Day 5: God of Forgiveness

> *Create in me a pure heart, O God, and renew a steadfast spirit within me. Do not cast me from your presence or take your Holy Spirit from me. Restore to me the joy of your salvation and grant me a willing spirit, to sustain me. (Psalm 51:10–12)*

King David is a wonderful example for us, as a man after God's own heart. He committed adultery with Bathsheba and had her husband killed, but when he came to his senses, aided by the prophet Nathan in 2 Samuel 12, David ran back to God to ask for forgiveness. And in that time of distress, he wrote Psalm 51.

Sin separates us from God because we allow it to. We act like Adam and Eve and hide because we know we have done wrong. When David sinned, he knew that the best thing for him was to turn back to God in repentance. He made a choice to return to God, because He knew His Heavenly Father would not send him away. David was a man after God's own heart. But that didn't make him perfect. But he knew that his perfect Father's love would result in forgiveness, if he humbled himself and admitted he had made an error of judgement.

Sometimes we try to grade our sins and maybe think that we haven't done anything as bad as David. But that isn't the way God sees things. God hates all sin, but thankfully He still loves the sinners.

We don't deserve to be welcomed back into God's presence, but Jesus has prepared the way for us by shedding His blood in payment for our sin. Such is God's love for us.

When we fall short of God's standards, He welcomes us back, time and time again. Even if we accidentally keep committing the same sin over and over again, feeling powerless to behave in a different way, we can still keep turning back to God in repentance. As we do that we give God permission to change our hearts towards the sin and eventually become free of it.

Let us be like David, who did not allow his failings to have a permanent effect on his relationship with God.

Daily Reading Plan Day 5: Exodus 10–11; Psalm 35.

Day 6: Approaching God our Father

Let us then approach God's throne of grace with confidence, so that we may receive mercy and find grace to help us in our time of need. (Hebrews 4:16)

God desires that we approach Him, the source of all that we need, so that we may discover how faithful He is. Although I had read the Bible sufficiently to know that in my head, my internal programming worked against that for many years (and still does from time to time!).

No matter how good our earthly fathers are, they are not perfect. As a result, we may attribute to God the things they taught us in error. When we have been programmed with those wrong ideas, it can take us many years to root them up replace them with the truth about God. Not least because we can be blissfully unaware that our thought processes are not reflecting what God teaches us in the Bible. Jesus said:

If you, then, though you are evil, know how to give good gifts to your children, how much more will your Father in heaven give good gifts to those who ask him! (Matthew 7:11)

We may think that we believe what the Bible says but remain unaware that the way we live our lives demonstrates we have failed to grasp its truth.

One thing which immediately springs to mind is that we may have been taught that we shouldn't do or say anything to upset other people. This seems like a good standard to live by. But when it comes to the practicality of life, we can find ourselves flattering others by telling "white lies" because we think God doesn't mind those. Sadly, we have missed the point that there aren't different coloured lies!

Ask the Holy Spirit to show you what beliefs are not in accordance with his teaching. Find Bible verses which reflect God's viewpoint. Meditate upon them and speak them out so that they will take root in your spirit and replace any wrong beliefs. It may take many years to discover and root all of them out. Be patient with yourself, but be determined to do it, so that you will more accurately reflect God's glory. Remember that if you ask God to help you with this, He will not fail you. He only knows how to give good gifts.

Daily Reading Plan Day 6: Exodus 12–13; Psalm 36.

Day 7: The Direct Route or the Scenic Route

It takes eleven days to go from Horeb to Kadesh Barnea by the Mount Seir road. (Deuteronomy 1:2)

Why did the Israelites take the scenic route from the Red Sea to the Jordan? It took them 40 years to finish a journey which could have taken 11 days!

If they knew in advance the consequences of their rebellion against God, I am sure that they would have wanted to make different choices. Then they would have made it to Canaan far more quickly! I think that they had lots of things to learn on the way.

I am reminded how children demonstrate their boredom on a journey as they often ask, "Are we nearly there yet?"

Sadly, the Israelites didn't consider the fact the journey could have taken less time. They obviously didn't enjoy the journey because they certainly did their share of complaining. They complained about not having anything to eat, asking if Moses had brought them out of Egypt to die. When God faithfully gave them manna to collect each morning, they complained that they didn't have any meat to eat. They also complained about not having water. They really tested Moses' patience – and God's!

Yet, sadly, the journey could have taken much less time if they had faced their trials with faith, instead of fear. They so easily forgot how God had brought them out of Egypt, parting the Red Sea for them and closing it again to destroy the Egyptians who were pursuing them.

It sounds to me like a dramatic event, which had the power to affect their response to future troubles. If God could part the Red Sea, surely they didn't need to be concerned about where their next meal was coming from? Yet they so easily forgot God's faithfulness.

We live in a world which is filled with worry, stress, and fear. Whether we are aware of it or not, we learn to respond the same way. Feed yourselves with the Word of God and allow your fear to be replaced by faith. God is faithful and can be trusted.

Daily Reading Plan Day 7: Exodus 14–15; Psalm 37.

Day 8: Why Take Risks?

> *You foolish person, do you want evidence that faith without deeds is useless? Was not our father Abraham considered righteous for what he did when he offered his son Isaac on the altar? You see that his faith and his actions were working together, and his faith was made complete by what he did. (James 2:20–22)*

If you want to walk on water, you have to get out of the boat. That's what Peter did. In Matthew 14:29, *"Then Peter got down out of the boat, walked on the water and came toward Jesus."* Okay, after a few steps he started to sink, but at least he stepped out in faith. Maybe we won't succeed the first time either, but it mustn't prevent us from exercising our faith.

It's so easy to think that Peter failed as he started to sink, but is that true? When we try something new, we don't often get it completely right first time. If we see that as failure, it will probably prevent us from having faith in God to help us with new things. But if we learn to celebrate small successes, we will be more likely to appreciate the benefits of exercising our faith in God.

As we succeed in the small steps, it will give us courage to take bigger steps of faith. As it is faith that pleases God, then He is going to be more pleased with us taking baby steps of faith, than not even getting out of the boat.

God loves us even if we stay in the boat. We don't need to earn His approval. But as we choose to put our trust in Him, it builds our relationship with Him. God doesn't just want us to do things for Him. He wants us to have a closer relationship with Him as we respond in faith. Faith in action builds our relationship with God.

In John's gospel, Jesus tells us that if we obey His command, we show that we love Him. So, it's necessary for us to be obedient to Him to demonstrate our love for Him. God is not trying to control us by asking us to do things, but He is inviting us into a love relationship with Him, as we choose to co-operate with His plans for our lives.

Pause for thought: What have you put off doing, for God, for far too long? Is now the time to make small or bigger steps of faith to begin to achieve the potential God has placed within you?

Daily Reading Plan Day 8: Exodus 16–17; Psalm 38.

Day 9: Turn Your Millstone into a Milestone

I can do all this through him who gives me strength. (Philippians 4:13)

How many people have you and I heard say that they want to lose weight or give up smoking? Maybe we have said things like that ourselves? It may be what we say we want, but unless that causes us to live differently, nothing will change.

My guess is that people say these things for many years before they actually do something about it. We need to move from a recognition that making changes would benefit us, to deciding that, "I want these benefits for myself, and I am prepared to do what it takes to make them happen!" We need to do something different.

Jesus tells us that as we follow Him, we can take His easy yoke, rather than it being a huge burden for us. But the enemy tries to convince us otherwise.

For too long I have procrastinated, because I have not believed I could do a task, forgetting that I am not supposed to achieve things on my own. The tasks are specifically designed for me, such that *I cannot* achieve them on my own. I was never meant to! It is about a partnership between me and God, as I respond to Him in faith.

Procrastination is a big enemy for us because we allow it to rob us of a better life – a life secure in our identity "in Christ," and the benefits He has purchased for us with His blood. Often we choose not to press on to the abundant life in Christ, because the change requires too much effort from us. If things don't change, and we haven't expended much effort, it seems better than making sacrifices and still failing! I understand that well.

If we allow procrastination to prevent us from doing God's will, it becomes a millstone to hold us back. But when we choose to break free, it becomes a milestone! It can help us to remember that in our weakness, Christ is our strength, but only if we choose to trust Him.

Daily Reading Plan Day 9: Exodus 18–19; Psalm 39.

Day 10: Finding God in the Trials of Life

Consider it pure joy, my brothers and sisters, whenever you face trials of many kinds, because you know that the testing of your faith produces perseverance. (James 1:2–3)

We face many trials in our lives, some short lived and some lasting much longer. We can even wonder whether God has gone to sleep or forgotten about us. But we read in Isaiah 49:15, *"Can a woman forget her sucking child, that she should have no compassion on the son of her womb? Even these may forget, but I will not forget you."*

This tells us that we can be absolutely sure that God hasn't forgotten us, even though if it feels that He has. Living by faith means that we are not being ruled by our feelings and by the things we can see. The circumstances of our lives may say one thing, but the truth about God can be totally different!

The more we get to know God, the more we can understand heaven's perspective of our trials and see the bigger picture. It's not always just about us. But when we are in difficult situations, we are more likely to consider how it affects us, rather than being able to see things from God's perspective. It takes time to develop a heavenly perspective, because we want things now, and do not want to wait for the spiritual fruit of patience. We can think that we are patient at times, but it may just be controlled impatience. (Think about that!)

When we demand to have our own way, we miss out. We may think that God has blessed us by answering our prayer, but we miss God's best plans for us. In a similar way, the Israelites kept asking God for a king, so that they would be like all the other nations (see 1 Samuel 8:19–20). God resisted, but they kept on asking. Eventually God gave then what they desired but told them they wouldn't like it!

Choose to see your trials as blessings, which can teach you more about yourself and also help you to learn the things which are most important to God.

Daily Reading Plan Day 10: Exodus 20–21; Psalm 40.

Day 11: Don't Forget God is Good!

> *But they soon forgot what he had done and did not wait for his plan to unfold. In the desert they gave in to their craving; in the wilderness they put God to the test. So he gave them what they asked for, but sent a wasting disease among them. (Psalm 106:13–15)*

The Israelites were in the wilderness and got fed up with eating manna, being ungrateful for it, because they wanted meat. They forgot that God had provided so many things for them and wanted the best for them. They didn't seek God or trust His timing, but continued demand meat. Psalm 106:15 says, *"He gave them what they asked, but sent a wasting disease among them."*

When we insist on having our way, rather than seeking God's will for our lives, we miss out on God's best for us, and settle for second best. When we do that, we are unwittingly siding with the enemy, who is trying to prevent us from having God's best. If we *really* knew that God wanted to give us His best, and imagined how good it would be, we surely wouldn't be prepared to settle for second best? But we live in a culture which wants things now. As a result, we allow the enemy to feed us with lies, rather than seeking God's truth.

The more we get to know God, forming an ever-deepening relationship with Him, the less likely we are to fall for Satan's lies. As we feed our minds with the truth in the Bible, the Holy Spirit will remind us of God's desires for our lives, which can help us to rise in faith and reject second best. Remember that anything which does not flow from faith in God is sin. Obviously, we can repent and choose to follow God's ways, but it doesn't automatically wipe out the consequences of our sin.

Abraham knew about that! He and his wife Sarai were childless, and Sarah was past the normal child-bearing age. But God spoke to him and told him that his descendants would be more numerous that the stars in the sky or the grains of sand on the sea shore, and that all the nations on the earth would be blessed through him. This was an amazing promise. Was this God? But Abram had a relationship with God, and knew His voice. He believed the promise and it was credited to him as righteousness.

Daily Reading Plan Day 11: Exodus 22–23; Psalm 41.

Day 12: Waiting for God's Timing

> *The Lord had said to Abram, "Go from your country, your people and your father's household to the land I will show you. "I will make you into a great nation, and I will bless you; I will make your name great, and you will be a blessing. I will bless those who bless you, and whoever curses you I will curse; and all peoples on earth will be blessed through you." (Genesis 12:1–3)*

God promised that Abram would have many descendants, but many years passed and there was still no sign of a baby, Abram and Sarai began to waiver in their faith. Maybe God meant that Abram was to be the father, but perhaps Sarai's maidservant, Hagar, should be the mother. So they took the short cut, and Hagar bore Abram a son called Ishmael when Abraham was 86 years old.

Thirteen years later God reminded Abram about the promise to make him a father of many nations and said that Sarai was to be the mother. If she was past child bearing age before, she certainly was now! But God said to change her name to Sarah (and Abram to Abraham) which would be a constant reminder for Him that God had intervened. God said that Sarah would bear a son the same time the following year, and that he should be called Isaac. And that's what happened.

Abraham's patience and faith in God had been tested. Similarly, when we are tested, often the last half mile seems the longest, and we can want to give up.

If God speaks to us about something He wants to do in our lives, it is so easy for us to think that it is going to happen soon, rather than 5, 10 or even 20 years later! God wants us to be spiritually prepared to receive our promises from Him. If we get too much success too soon, we can fall into the trap of thinking that we did it on our own. But the longer we are required to wait, the more we know that we cannot achieve it on our own. That way, when it eventually happens, we will give God the glory.

That's what happened when Isaac was born. There was no way that Sarah would have been able to bring forth a child when she was so old. But God did what only He can do! He really is a God of the impossible.

Daily Reading Plan Day 12: Exodus 24–25; Psalm 42.

Day 13: How Long, Lord?

Oh, that you would rend the heavens and come down, that the mountains would tremble before you! (Isaiah 64:1)

We can hear people speak about God's timing as though it were a date on the calendar, without fully realising that we have a part to play. Playing the waiting game is not a passive thing. It requires praying, reading the Bible, listening to the Holy Spirit and being obedient at the right time. It can also include speaking out God's plans for our life, when the enemy tries to steal them from us. Then amazingly, at the right time, things seem to happen suddenly!

If we are slow to allow God's character to be formed in us, it delays the promises being fulfilled, and can take 40 years to do an 11-day journey, as it did with the Israelites.

As we wait, the knowledge of God's plans for our lives can assist us in making life-changing decisions and may prevent us from making choices which will delay the timing of God's promise. If we ask the Holy Spirit to guide us each day, and follow His directions, we will obtain our promises from God quicker. Sometimes, like Abraham, we can try to 'help' God. However, the shortest route isn't always the best route, which we can discover to our peril.

But we cannot afford to be passive and think that if God wants to do something in our lives, that it will just happen, without any co-operation on our part. The enemy would love us to believe that lie. We need to take God's Words to us seriously and ask God to open opportunities for us to co-operate with Him. If we do that, then He will take our words seriously. That is how relationships work. Do you have any promises or dreams from God which haven't been fulfilled yet? Have you just put them on the shelf and waited for God to do it? Or maybe you tried to help Him and things went wrong?

What is your next step? Take some time to prayerfully consider your next course of action. When you play your part, it releases God to play His.

Daily Reading Plan Day 13: Exodus 26–27; Psalm 43.

Day 14: God is on Your Side

> *No weapon forged against you will prevail, and you will refute every tongue that accuses you. This is the heritage of the servants of the Lord, and this is their vindication from me," declares the Lord. (Isaiah 54:17)*

Sometimes we come to a place where we feel we are totally blocked and find it difficult to move forward to achieve our goals. It may happen because the enemy is trying to prevent us from doing what God wants us to do. Sometimes it is God getting in the way! It is not always obvious at first, and I have found myself saying "Either this is very right, or very wrong."

I am at one of those very places as a write as I am in the process of moving to a new house. Until yesterday, everything was going well. There had been a few holdups along the way, but nothing of any great concern. Suddenly, yesterday, my vendor decided that she no longer wants to move to a new house, just when we were poised to exchange contracts.

I was faced with a choice. Do I get upset and angry with her or do I look to God for His guidance? I chose to look to God, who can see the big picture, and praise Him because His Word says that He *"works for the good of those who love Him, who have been called according to His purpose"* (Romans 8:28). Whatever happens, God is on my side, as I look to Him for guidance, and choose to be obedient.

At this moment I do not know whether I will be moving next week, in a couple of months, or not at all. But it doesn't matter. I don't need to get upset about this because God is working for me. There is no benefit to complaining, as that displays a lack of faith in God. The news was a real surprise to me but it wasn't news to God. He knows the end from the beginning so providing I stay close to Him, all will be well.

It may seem a though I am being passive and fatalistic. But that is not the case. I am praising God for His faithfulness to me and His ability to do the impossible. I am choosing to worship the author and perfecter of my faith who will bring me through to the other side. I am praying in the spirit so that I may connect with the will of God, that my prayers will be answered. I really do not know what the outcome will be, but I am at peace. Praise God!

Daily Reading Plan Day 14: Exodus 28–29; Psalm 44.

Day 15: Give Way or Stop?

> *Then Moses stretched out his hand over the sea, and all that night the Lord drove the sea back with a strong east wind and turned it into dry land. The waters were divided. (Exodus 14:21)*

The Israelites had visible evidence of God's presence with them so that they knew when to stay and when to move on. When we have something blocking our way, we need to listen to the Holy Spirit to hear whether He is saying "stop," or whether we need to approach the situation as "give way," being ready to move when the way is clear.

Let's look at Abraham again. God eventually gave Him a son, Isaac, who he treasured as a gift from God. Isaac was the one to continue the family line and play his part in history. And yet God told him to take Isaac up to Mount Moriah and sacrifice him to God.

Now God had already said He did not approve of child sacrifice, which was the practice for worshipping other gods. But nevertheless, God had told him to go up the mountain with Isaac for that purpose, and to sacrifice the one who was destined to give him many descendants. Abraham didn't understand, but he was obedient and trusted that God knew what He was doing. When it came to the moment of Abraham murdering his precious son, God blocked the way, showing Abraham the ram caught in the thicket, which would be the sacrifice.

In humility Abraham gave way to God, trusting that He had a plan. In a similar way, we need to trust God's plan for our lives, listening carefully to each prompting we receive from the Holy Spirit. To be more attentive to the Spirit, we are wise to ask to be filled afresh each day. Receiving the Holy Spirit is not intended to be a one-off event.

I have heard people say the we need to be re-filled because the problem is that we leak. However, I would dare to suggest that we don't leak enough! Each time we follow His guidance and act in His power, we create further capacity for Him to fill us again.

Daily Reading Plan Day 15: Exodus 30–31; Psalm 45.

Day 16: Faith or Sin?

> *"But my righteous one shall live by faith, And I take no pleasure in the one who shrinks back." (Hebrews 10:38)*

It may seem strange to suggest that faith and sin are opposites. If we were asked for the opposite of faith, we might say, "unbelief." But most of us wouldn't say that it is sin.

Yet the Bible tells us that, *"everything that does not come from faith is sin"* (Romans 14:23). Romans 6:23 says, *"the wages of sin is death,"* whilst Galatians 3:11 has, *"Clearly no one who relies on the law is justified before God, because 'the righteous will live by faith.'"*

Romans 14:23 in the Amplified Bible further explains *"for whatever doesn't originate and proceed from faith is sin (whatever is done without a conviction of the approval of God, is sinful)."*

This tells us that in order not to sin, we need to believe that God approves of what we are planning to do. Having believed that, we can act on it.

When we are fairly new Christians we do not know God very well, and do not yet know much of the Bible, and as a result we can do things unwittingly, which wouldn't have God's approval. In that situation God is more lenient with us. On that basis, we may think that it will be best to keep our heads down and not learn God's ways! Surely that way we can get away with anything?

As we come to know more of God's ways, through prayer, reading the Bible, and the guidance of the Holy Spirit, we become more accountable for our actions. As it says in the Bible, *"Whoever knows what is right to do and fails to do it, for him it is sin"* (James 4:17).

But having accepted the free gift of salvation, through Christ's death, motivated by His love for us, how can we not love Him and want to please Him in return? And anyway, one of the most basic commands is to love the Lord your God, with all your heart, soul, and mind.

Daily Reading Plan Day 16: Exodus 32–33; Psalm 46.

Day 17: Choose Life

> *See, I set before you today life and prosperity, death and destruction. 16 For I command you today to love the Lord your God, to walk in obedience to him, and to keep his commands, decrees and laws; then you will live and increase, and the Lord your God will bless you in the land you are entering to possess. (Deuteronomy 30:15)*

As we grasp more of the concept that God loves us, we need for our own good, to spend time finding out how He would like us to live, so that we will experience the abundant life which Jesus has paid for.

Looking again at Romans 6:23, we are told that, *"the wages of sin is death, but the gift of God is eternal life in Christ Jesus our Lord."* That says that if we sin, we earn the death penalty, but by God's grace all who turn to Jesus, putting their trust in Him, will be saved from that penalty.

Sinners sitting on death row still have the option to turn to God. By His grace, He still loves the sinners, even though they may not be able to respond to His love. God longs for them to turn to Jesus in faith, accepting the sacrifice He made for them. When that happens, the spiritual death sentence is pronounced null and void, even though their physical bodies may die. At that point, they begin eternal life, starting on earth.

By faith the sinner, who repents, and turns to God, is no longer viewed by God as a sinner. Jesus demonstrated this when he told one of the criminals being crucified with him that they would be together in Paradise.

Colossians 1:13 says, *"For he has rescued us from the dominion of darkness and brought us into the kingdom of the Son he loves."* Such an amazing transaction takes place when we choose Jesus. How can we not respond in love to Him?

Each of us has the opportunity to choose the abundant life, which Jesus has bought for us. We don't just drift into it by accident. We need to make a choice.

Daily Reading Plan Day 17: Exodus 34–35; Psalm 47.

Day 18: God Honours Those Who Honour Him

Therefore the Lord, the God of Israel, declares: 'I promised that members of your family would minister before me forever.' But now the Lord declares: 'Far be it from me! Those who honour me I will honour, but those who despise me will be disdained. (1 Samuel 2:30)

At the New Wine Conference in 2012, I heard a wonderful testimony by one of the main speakers, Francis Chan, who said that after he had been married for a few months his wife asked him whether she did anything which annoyed him. He mentioned a few things and then felt obliged to ask her the same question. He cynically thought that she was trying to contrive a situation so that she could tell him about things which upset her!

However, over the next few months, he discovered that she stopped doing the things which annoyed him. She loved him so much that she wanted to stop doing the things which he didn't like.

Is that how it is for us and God? Do we love Him so much that we would choose to stop doing the things which he doesn't like? Also, do we choose to do the things that He does want us to do?

I, personally, find that very challenging. It's not that I deliberately do things He doesn't like, but I can seriously procrastinate at times over things He has asked me to do. It's not that I am being deliberately awkward, but I have difficulty fully engaging with His purpose for me doing those things.

Sometimes we just need to be obedient to God's Word even though we may not fully understand why. I have discovered that it may take a very long time to understand why we have been instructed to do something, or we may never know during our time on this earth. But John's gospel tells us that the ones who love God are the ones who are obedient to him.

Do we choose to honour Him by being obedient in all areas of our lives? Do we love Him that much?

Daily Reading Plan Day 18: Exodus 36–37; Psalm 48.

Day 19: A Costly Sacrifice

"Enlarge the place of your tent, stretch your tent curtains wide, do not hold back; lengthen your cords, strengthen your stakes. For you will spread out to the right and to the left; your descendants will dispossess nations and settle in their desolate cities. (Isaiah 54:2–3)

This speaks of enlarging our imaginations to be able to receive the greatness of God's plans for us. We are encouraged to engage with the Holy Spirit such that we may see more clearly with our spiritual eyes.

How willing are we to seek God's perspective of our lives? How much do we love Him, so that we desire to receive, by faith, the things He wants to give us? Are we prepared to pay the cost, in time and energy, to engage with God's plan for our lives? Will we meditate on the vision God gives us, bringing it into a spiritual reality? We also need to speak it out. Remember that in the book of Genesis, God imagined the world and spoke it into being. If that is how it worked for God, how can it be any different for us, who are created in God's image?

Jesus was prepared to pay the cost for us. He paid with His very life-blood, to bring us salvation, healing, deliverance, and abundant provision. By God's grace these blessings are available to us. We cannot earn them. They are free. But they are not cheap. Jesus paid the price for them with His very life-blood. A costly sacrifice to provide precious gifts. Do we so value these gifts that we are willing to seek God with all our hearts, so that we may receive all that Jesus has paid for?

Romans 12:2 says to *"be transformed by the renewing of your mind, so that you will be able to prove God's good, perfect and acceptable will."* As we educate our minds with the things of God, it builds faith in us to believe that what God says, is true.

We then see our lives changed, such that we have proof that it is true. It is a life-long process, it doesn't happen overnight The more we choose to live by faith in the Word of God (the Bible), made flesh (Jesus), the more we enter into the abundant life which He has purchased for us by His blood. God is amazing!

Daily Reading Plan Day 19: Exodus 38–39; Psalm 49.

Day 20: Desire Solid Food

> *For though by this time you ought to be teachers, you need someone yet again to teach you the first principles of God's Word. You still need milk, not solid food; for everyone who lives on milk is unskilled in the Word of righteousness, for he is like a child. But solid food is for the mature, for those who have their faculties trained by practice to distinguish good from evil. (Hebrews 5:12–14)*

This is quite a tough passage. The writer is telling us that some people continue as baby Christians, because they have not allowed God's word and their life's experiences to train them to know the difference between good and evil. They still require milk and not the food you have to chew and work at. They have not discovered that they have a role to play in the kingdom of God; a role in which they need to take some responsibility in passing on the love of God to others in such a way that it transforms them. We have been called to make a difference in this world!

Romans 8:19 says that all of creation is waiting for the sons of God to be revealed. It is true that we need to come to our Heavenly Father as children, trusting and teachable, looking to Him to provide for all our needs. But whilst we retain these characteristics, we also need to mature in the Word of God and grow up into sons of God.

I believe that if every Christian grew up to be a son of God, the world would be a very different place to live. When this happens, we discover the plans and purposes God has for our lives. As we then work in co-operation with Him, moving in the authority Jesus has delegated to us, we see power of the Holy Spirit displayed.

Sometimes we mistakenly believe that God's plans for our lives are for our satisfaction. Whilst it says in Jeremiah 29:11–13 that His plans are for our welfare, which suggests they will be good for us, nevertheless the plans are not solely for us. As each of us plays the part God has apportioned to us, we work as a team and are inter-dependent, so that God alone gets the glory!

Daily Reading Plan Day 20: Leviticus 1–2; Psalm 50.

Day 21: Adopted into God's Family?

> *In love he predestined us for adoption to sonship through Jesus Christ, in accordance with his pleasure and will— to the praise of his glorious grace, which he has freely given us in the One he loves. (Ephesians 1:5–6)*

In Luke 15 we learn the parable which is known as "The Prodigal Son." The younger son effectively wished his father dead, because he asked for his share of the inheritance before his father died. Amazingly, his father agreed to it.

The son went off and squandered the money on wild living and then found himself penniless, having nothing to eat. As a Jew, the pigs were regarded as unclean animals, but he was so desperate that he took a job feeding pigs. Not only that, but he had to eat the same food as the pigs. How humiliating.

When he came to his senses, he decided to go back home and ask his father for a job, because he knew his father's employees were treated well. So, he travelled back home, preparing himself to admit that he had sinned against God and against his father. But his father saw him as he approached and ran to meet him. He celebrated his return by killing the fatted calf and re-instated him as a son.

The older son was not happy about this because he didn't get that response from his father. But he had never asked to have a party! In fact, he hadn't drawn anything at all from his close relationship with his father. Instead, he viewed his work as slaving for his father, because he could not see any benefits.

If he had chosen to see his father differently, he would have seen a man who was generous and gracious. Instead of feeling blessed by having such a wonderful father, he chose to feel like a slave, and behave like one.

The younger son clearly got things wrong initially, but he chose to learn from his experiences, so that he could come to his father in humility. His father knew that his son must have learned a few lessons while he was away, or he wouldn't have come back home. Therefore, it was worth celebrating his son's return, because it showed that he had increased in maturity.

Daily Reading Plan Day 21: Leviticus 3–4; Psalm 51.

Day 22: Victim or Victor?

> *As it is written: "For your sake we face death all day long; we are considered as sheep to be slaughtered." No, in all these things we are more than conquerors through him who loved us. (Romans 8:36–37)*

Following on from the parable of the Prodigal Son, how do we respond to life's challenges? Do we moan and blame everyone else, seeing our cup as only half empty? Or do we see that our response to life's challenges influences the outcome? Can we be mature enough to learn from our mistakes and choose to behave differently? Can we even feel blessed if our cup is only half full?

In short, are we prepared to take some responsibility for our lives? When we do that, we are no longer victims, but people who can make wise choices. If we not only let our experiences teach us but are also prepared to learn from the Word of God, and godly wisdom of others, it shows we have moved from being infants in Christ, to mature sons of God.

We no longer need the 'milky' foundational teachings. But we can chew and digest the meat of God's Word, which leads to greater maturity.

Take time to think about your life. Are you beaten under the circumstances of your life, or can you see your life from heaven's perspective, having vision that you have the power to change your circumstances by making wise choices? Ask the Holy Spirit to show you if any situations cause you to think like a victim, rather than rising up and becoming victorious?

What wise choices can you make, to change the outcome of your life? I once heard a wise man of God say, "You are only one decision away from your breakthrough." At that time, I felt beaten by circumstances and felt offended by what he said. But, as time progressed I realised that what he said was the truth.

The Bible tells us that we are the head and not the tail (Deut 28:13) and that we have the mind of Christ (1 Cor 2:16). Therefore, we are not victims and we have the capacity to rise above our circumstances.

Daily Reading Plan Day 22: Leviticus 5–6; Psalm 52.

Day 23: The Possible or The Impossible

Jesus looked at them and said, "With man this is impossible, but with God all things are possible." (Matthew 19:23)

I have a wonderfully entertaining book, written by an American international speaker and author, Cathy Lechner, entitled, "I Hope God's Promises Come to Pass Before My Body Parts Go South" (Charisma Media, 1998). Although it is written in a light-hearted way, it has a very serious message.

I have read, and re-read this book several times, and I have found it to be very helpful. She introduced me to a new way of looking at things: either they are possible or impossible.

She writes about an encounter with God, where she was told that she was living in the possible. As an international speaker, wife, and mother, she must juggle so many things in order to travel for God. But God said that she was living in the possible and challenged her to step into the impossible.

Initially, when she heard God speak to her, she assumed that it must be a word of encouragement. But then He pointed out that it was a word of rebuke!

What would God say about our lives? Are we just living in the possible, such that if the Spirit departed from us we wouldn't notice the difference?

Or we may have stepped out in faith, doing what God has asked us to do. At the beginning, we may have been well out of our comfort zone. But as time progressed, that which was originally impossible for us without God's help, has become comfortable and feels "possible" for us to do without God's help any more. When that happens, we need to be stretched again.

Ask God to challenge you again. Dare to be obedient and to step out into the impossible again, knowing that with Him, all things become possible.

Daily Reading Plan Day 23: Leviticus 7–8; Psalm 53.

Day 24: Dare to Dream Big Dreams

> *See, I am doing a new thing! Now it springs up; do you not perceive it? (Isaiah 43:19)*

I have heard it said that if our dreams and visions for our lives don't scare us, then they aren't from God.

God calls us to step out of the "possible," where we can manage without Him, and into the "impossible," where we cannot succeed without His help. At times like these, we learn to lean on Him, asking Him to undertake what only He can do.

When things are impossible for us, we turn to the Lord of the impossible. When He is Lord, the impossible becomes possible. When we surrender to Him as Lord of our lives, He enables us to do what is impossible for us on our own. We play our part, and God does His. Great teamwork!

Will we look at the giants and say "The opposition is too great!" (Numbers 13), or will we face the giants head on, believing that God will help us succeed? Will we respond in fear or faith?

Do you have dreams for your life, which seem to be too big to even try? Does it seem ridiculous to even attempt them? Imagine them for a moment (take your time). You know you can't achieve them on your own, so who would get the glory? Dare to believe that these ideas are from God, and you are not just having a funny 5 minutes!

God plan for us is bigger than ourselves. His plan is for us to share His love and His glory with the people He puts in our lives. His purposes for our lives are not so that we will succeed, but so that we can help others to succeed. Jesus gave His life for us, so that we can give our lives to others.

If every one of us were to just live our lives in our comfort zone, God's purposes would not be fulfilled. The reality is that if we choose not to engage with God's plan, someone else will. Many are called but few are chosen, because few of us say "Yes" to God's call, and are willing to submit to His authority.

Daily Reading Plan Day 24: Leviticus 9–10; Psalm 54.

Day 25: He Gives us Our Desires

Take delight in the Lord and He will give you the desires of your heart. (Psalm 37:4)

God created each one of us, so He knows how we are wired. He knows what would bring us fulfilment and satisfaction. He knows our desires, because He put them there. So therefore, He gives us the desires which He puts in our heart, and as we trust Him, and co-operate with Him, He fulfils them. It sounds simple, but it often doesn't work out quite as easily as that.

We have an enemy, who will do all he can to steal, kill and destroy. I have heard of so many Christians who say that they don't believe we have an enemy, even the devil/Satan, yet the Bible teaches us that we do. Just because people don't believe in the devil doesn't mean he doesn't exist.

The enemy sees our potential, and attacks those very areas which, if submitted to God, would bring God glory. There is no point in attacking something which is never going to produce fruit for God. The enemy would just be wasting his energy.

So, what are the battles you are facing in your life? What is the enemy trying to sabotage?

Andrew Wommack once said that if you are not experiencing opposition from the enemy, you and he are walking in the same direction! Whilst I wouldn't put it that strongly, I do believe that the closer we are to fulfilling God's plans for our lives, the more obstacles the devil puts in our way. Ultimately, he won't win, but he will do all he can to try to throw us off course.

Have you unwittingly allowed Satan to disrupt God's plan for your life? If that is true, all is not lost. Ask God to re-ignite your desires for Him. With the new knowledge of the enemy at work, choose not to let him steal from you. Whenever he feeds you lies, choose not to believe them, and replace them with truths within the Bible. Remember, you are on the winning side. Anyone wholeheartedly working on God's team has to overcome the enemy (1 John 2:14; 4:4)! Just keep believing the truth!

Daily Reading Plan Day 25: Leviticus 11–12; Psalm 55.

Day 26: Put on God's Whole Armour

> *Finally, be strong in the Lord and in his mighty power.* [11] *Put on the full armor of God, so that you can take your stand against the devil's schemes. (Ephesians 6:10–11)*

Will you put on the whole armour of God (see Ephesians 6), and believing God's truth, stand firm? As you stand up for the truth of God's Word, He credits that faith to you as righteousness. If you stand up to be counted on God's team, you are on the winning side. The impossible has already become possible. By God's grace we partake of the privilege of being seated in heavenly places with Christ Jesus (Eph 2:6), where we can see life from heaven's perspective, in the knowledge that we already have the victory.

That doesn't mean that Satan gives up and goes home straight away, but at some point, he will realise that his efforts to steal from us are futile.

When the going gets tough, many people give up. They are not prepared to persist against such resistance. But the greater the resistance, the closer we are to victory. We are already connected with victory in the spirit realm, and our faith in the unseen will soon cause the victory to be seen.

In Hebrews 10, there is a reward for those who endure, for God has pleasure in the ones who continue in faith to the end. If we do not persist till the end, we will not receive the prize which is waiting for us.

So what will we do? Will we give up before the end? Or will we persist until we see the victory, and see the impossible happen?

James 4:7 tells us that as we resist the devil, by faith in Jesus, he will flee from us.

Our victory is not only achieved by our persistence, but also by engaging with God's timing. As we invite the Holy Spirit to refill us daily, we can be more sensitive to this, and ultimately see God's glory revealed.

Daily Reading Plan Day 26: Leviticus 13–14; Psalm 56.

Day 27: The Lord is Great!

> *But may all who seek you rejoice and be glad in you; may those who long for your saving help always say, "The Lord is great!" (Psalm 40:16)*

In John 21 we read about Peter and some of the other disciples going fishing together after Jesus' death. They had fished all night but had caught nothing. They knew that fishing at night was the most productive, but it hadn't worked for them.

At daybreak Jesus arrived and told them to cast their net on the other side of the boat, which would have made no sense to these experienced fishermen. But being obedient, they were rewarded with many fish! They connected with Jesus' timing and then the thing which had seemed impossible was suddenly possible. It made no logical sense, but it worked!

Have you felt prompted by God to do something which didn't make sense to your natural mind? Does a certain thought come to mind, repeatedly, and won't go away? Are you questioning whether God may be speaking to you, but you are uncertain?

I have discovered for myself that some of the strangest ideas can be from God. Who gets the glory if the idea is successful? God, you, or the enemy?

If the thoughts go against what the Bible teaches, they are to be discarded. If you feel that you have achieved something amazing, in your own strength, then they are probably your ideas. But if you know that you cannot perform this task on your own, so that God would get the glory, it is probably Him speaking to you.

It is wise to ask the opinion of a Christian whose view you respect, maybe your church leader. However, ultimately, you need to be at complete peace to move forward. Not the sort of peace which you get when you are in your comfort zone, but the peace which passes understanding and can only come from God.

Daily Reading Plan Day 27: Leviticus 15–16; Psalm 57.

Day 28: Knowing the Truth Can Set You Free

> *To the Jews who had believed him, Jesus said, "If you hold to my teaching, you are really my disciples. Then you will know the truth, and the truth will set you free." (John 8:32)*

The enemy exists! He is an expert deceiver, and therefore the last thing he wants us to know is the truth! Yet the Bible tells us that it is important for us to know the truth, because then we can be set free.

The problem many of us have is that we think we already know the truth. I was speaking to someone only yesterday about God's love for her, and she replied, "I already know that!"

Thankfully she listened to my reply. "We can know things in our head, but it is only when we know them in our heart that our lives are changed by them." Colossians 3:16 says we must let the Word of God dwell richly in us.

I believe that that means that we feel blessed by knowing the Word of God when we can see its fruit in our lives. When we hear a familiar passage of scripture or hear someone say something that we have heard before, we need to check whether that word is having an impact and has found its home within us. Is it something we just know in our minds, or have we allowed it to transform us?

In various places in the Bible we can read the words, "whoever has ears to hear, let them hear" (e.g. Luke 8:8). We also read that people can have the ability to hear, but they do not actually listen and register the words being spoken.

God spoke to me many years ago that, "If my people really knew how much I loved them, they would be different." It was certainly true for me at the time, and even years later, it is probably still true for me to some degree.

Do you really know that God loves you passionately? You are the apple of His eye and He delights to spend time with you. Allow that realisation to really take root in you, so that it informs the way you speak and act.

Daily Reading Plan Day 28: Leviticus 17–18; Psalm 58.

Day 29: An Overflowing Heart

> *A good man brings good things out of the good stored up in his heart, and an evil man brings evil things out of the evil stored up in his heart. For the mouth speaks what the heart is full of. (Luke 6:45)*

Some other translations of the Bible record that 'out the overflow of the heart the mouth speaks'.

When you are feeling stressed or under pressure, what comes out of your mouth? Is it self-effacing? Do you curse God? Do you blame other people?

When Adam had been found out by God, that he had eaten the fruit of the forbidden tree, he blamed Eve. Eve blamed the serpent.

Some of us think we are always at fault. Some of us blame other people of God.

We can be prone to apologising afterwards, saying that we didn't really mean those unkind words. But if we said them, we meant them! We may not have meant to say them, but they do reflect what is in our heart.

It is so easy to forget that Romans 8:28 tells us that God works all things for the good for those who love Him and are called according to His purpose.

Listen to yourself as you speak. Do not dismiss your words too speedily. Maybe write things down if you don't have time to think about them straight away. Ask the Holy Spirit to help you understand why you say what you do.

These are some of the questions you could consider:

> Are you being unkind to yourself or other people?
>
> Are you unable to forgive yourself or other people?
>
> Are you trying to control situations and insist on them being done your way?
>
> Do you not believe that God will provide for all your needs?

Ask God to guide you to relevant verses in the Bible can help you to change what is in your heart. Only then can you really love others and love yourself.

Daily Reading Plan Day 29: Leviticus 19–20; Psalm 59.

Day 30: Do not Judge Others

> *Do not judge, or you too will be judged. For in the same way you judge others, you will be judged, and with the measure you use, it will be measured to you.* (Matthew 7:1–2)

As a human race we are good at pointing out the faults of others, in the very areas where we are failing. Yet we seem unaware that we, too, need to change. Each time you find yourself being critical of someone else, ask the Holy Spirit to show you whether you are also getting that thing wrong. Then when we have had the plank removed from our eye, we will be able to someone else remove the speck from theirs.

I remember hearing a young man at church say that whilst he was at university, a good friend had called him a "plank-eyed speck picker." That phrase has amused me ever since!

As we become more aware of our own frailty, it enables us to see others from the same perspective, so that we can more easily forgive others when they do hurtful things. The more we discover of God's love for us, the more able we are to know how to love and respect others, in that same manner. This enables us to show grace to others and to become peacemakers, which is what God asks us to do. This sort of peace is not pretending that nothing is wrong but being able to admit that wrong has been done, without holding it against our neighbours.

Such humility helps us to see other people from God's perspective; that of unconditional love. As we trust our lives into God's hands, we no longer need to be on control, because we discover that God can do a much better job than we can on our own!

Romans 12:18 instructs us to live peaceably with all, if possible, so far as it depends on us. As we make peace our aim, it will give God the opportunity to work things out the best way, so that He will receive the glory. When we struggle to do, or say, the things that bring peace, we can remind ourselves of Philippians 4:13, *"I can do all this through him who gives me strength."*

Daily Reading Plan Day 30: Leviticus 21–22; Psalm 60.

Day 31: God Provides for all my Needs

The Lord is my shepherd, I lack nothing. He makes me lie down in green pastures, he leads me beside quiet waters, he refreshes my soul. He guides me along the right paths for his name's sake. (Psalm 23:1–3)

Psalm 23 tells us 'The Lord is my shepherd. I shall nothing lack.' This says that as we choose to follow Jesus, He will provide for all our needs. Do you believe that?

I firmly believe that it is true, although I have struggled to see it as a reality in my life. For many years I had been in want financially, but I came to realise that it's not the result of God's lack of faithfulness to me, but my lack of faithfulness to God.

It can be helpful to look at 1 Kings 17 and read about God's provision for Elijah. Firstly, God told him to go to the Kerith brook, where the ravens fed him. Secondly, he was instructed to go to meet a widow in Zarapheth, who God used to feed him. God told Elijah to go, in both cases. As a result, he received God's provision. If he had chosen to stay where he was, he would not have been fed, because God had arranged for the provision to be in a different place.

If we are struggling to make ends meet financially, we can benefit considerably by spending time with God in prayer, asking Him whether anything in our lives needs to be adjusted for us to receive all that we need. It could be as simple as spending too much on an extravagant lifestyle or giving away money that we do not have. Maybe God is trying to say something? Are we listening?

For many years I have struggled because I have been unwilling to write this book! It was in 1996 that God first told me to write. Initially I was obedient. But my first attempt at publishing a book was unsuccessful, which caused me to give up. Over the years I have tried writing, but then destroyed my work because I thought it wasn't good enough. That disobedience blocked God's provision!

Daily Reading Plan Day 31: Leviticus 23–24; Psalm 61.

Day 32: Submit to God

> *Humble yourselves, therefore, under God's mighty hand, that he may lift you up in due time. (1 Peter 5:6)*

Sometimes we can procrastinate for many years, because we cannot see the purpose in being obedient to God. It's not so much that we are being obstructive, but we cannot grasp the vision for doing it. So, we don't feel motivated. For some of us, we are concerned that we may fail in the new venture and we don't want to be seen to fail. Somehow, by not even attempting the task, we can feel less of a failure than if we were obedient and it didn't work out the way we planned.

We can miss the point that God has plans that depend on our obedience, and not our being successful in the world's eyes. He doesn't just ask us to do something on a whim! As we choose to do what God is asking, we begin to humble ourselves before God, so that it gives God the opportunity to raise us up, in His good timing. Humility always results in being blessed.

> *But he gives us more grace. That is why Scripture says: "God opposes the proud but shows favour to the humble." Submit yourselves, then, to God. Resist the devil, and he will flee from you. (James 4:6–7)*

When we procrastinate because we cannot understand the point of being obedient to God, it shows that we are proud. We will only do what we think is important. God opposes the proud.

When we choose to be obedient to God, it says that we place a high value on His views, whether we understand them. The important thing is honouring God, in submission to His will. What we want pales into insignificance when compared to the desires of our God.

We are called to follow Jesus, who came to this earth and suffered immeasurable pain, not because it was what He wanted, but because others would benefit. If we are called to follow Him, we are called to a life lived for the benefit of others – the road less travelled.

Daily Reading Plan Day 32: Leviticus 25–26; Psalm 62.

Day 33: God's Kingdom First

> *But seek first his kingdom and his righteousness, and all these things will be given to you as well. Therefore, do not worry about tomorrow, for tomorrow will worry about itself. Each day has enough trouble of its own. (Matthew 6:33–34)*

God delights in providing for all our needs. Of course, we cannot snap our fingers and have everything we want, just at the time we want it. If it were that simple, we would miss out on the joy of having a loving relationship with our Father.

But God is trustworthy, and if He says He is our provider, we need to believe Him, and put our trust in Him. However, if we have a good job, a lovely house and other possessions, we can fall into the trap of thinking that since we earned the money, it all belongs to us. We can miss the point that God provided the job for us and gave us the ability to do the work.

When we receive our salary at the end of the month, we would do well to thank God for His provision and to ask for guidance to spend it wisely, thereby putting God and His kingdom first. In reality, most of the money is probably ear-marked for the monthly standing orders and direct debits, but we are wise to follow God's direction with regard to giving to others, even sacrificially, as He directs.

Whenever we give for the purposes of God's Kingdom, we are to do it unbegrudgingly and with a cheerful heart, so that our requests may be heard in heaven. As we do that, we are effectively making an investment into our heavenly bank account, sowing into God's Kingdom, so that we may reap a harvest at due time.

Our motivation must not be so that we receive it back with interest. However, what farmer has ever sowed any seed, with the purpose of letting it die in the ground, and not being of benefit to him? It is a great privilege to have the ability to invest in heaven's economy, to help others, and to know that when we are in need, God won't allow us to starve. We serve a generous God, who provides for us abundantly, but our focus must always be on the giver of the blessings, rather than the blessings themselves.

Daily Reading Plan Day 33: Leviticus 27; Psalm 63.

Day 34: No Condemnation

> *Therefore, there is now no condemnation for those who are in Christ Jesus, because through Christ Jesus the law of the Spirit who gives life has set you[a] free from the law of sin and death. (Romans 8:1–2)*

If we have chosen to follow Christ and have His Spirit living within us, we have the privilege of having access to the abundant life which Jesus has bought for us (see John 10:10).

We know that we have sinned and fallen short of the glory of God, but Jesus has stepped in and paid for that sin with His blood, so that our "slate" has been wiped clean. Even though we know our history, God no longer chooses to see our sin because He has removed it as far as east is from west. That sounds great in theory, but why do we continue to feel guilty?

We have an enemy who delights in reminding us of our sin and causes us to feel condemned because he knows the guilt we feel will prevent us from moving forward into God's purposes. "Who are we to think that God will use us?" the enemy asks.

Sadly, we can succumb to such taunting and allow it to get in the way of our serving God. If we allow ourselves to believe such lies, they become giants which prevent us from inheriting our promised land. Do you remember that when the spies were sent to check out the promised land, most of them came back telling about the giants who lived there? They came back in fear, rather than seeing that God was planning to give them great victories.

We have a choice. Either we can bow to the threat of the giants in our lives, or we can step forward in faith, being willing to do all God asks of us; not because we have earned the right to be used of God—but trusting in the power of the finished work of Jesus.

Jesus died and rose again, showing that sin and death could not hold him. As we put our trust in Jesus, we have access to the same resurrection power, by claiming the righteousness which Jesus bought for us. There is no condemnation for those who are in Christ Jesus!

Daily Reading Plan Day 34: Numbers 1–2; Psalm 64.

Day 35: Life in the Spirit

Those who live according to the flesh have their minds set on what the flesh desires; but those who live in accordance with the Spirit have their minds set on what the Spirit desires. The mind governed by the flesh is death, but the mind governed by the Spirit is life and peace. (Romans 8:5–6)

In reality, most Christians are not wholly set towards the things of the Spirit. Our desire should be to set our minds on the things of the Spirit, so that we may live our lives the way God intends. We may be able to manage this on Sundays when we have been to church. But what happens on Mondays when get to work and face all sorts of problems, and other people whose aim is not to live by God's guidance?

If we aren't able to live by the Spirit on Mondays, do we just forget God until the next Sunday? Is it even possible to live our life in the Spirit, or is it just being idealistic?

If we look again at the passage from Romans 8, I think that the key word is SET your minds on things above. Setting our minds in that way is about making a choice to see our lives from a heavenly perspective. It relates to a choice to read the Bible, pray and follow the guidance of the Holy Spirit.

We may get side-tracked from time to time. But when we do, we need to re-set our rudder so that the course of our life is directed towards God. The more often we choose to do that, the easier it will become, and eventually it will be our automatic default when the circumstances of life threaten to take us off course.

Choose to see heaven as your treasure and your heart will follow suit. It takes determination and perseverance because at first it will seem very unnatural to us. But if our desire is to engage with the fulfilling, abundant life which is available to us, we must be single minded.

The rubbish of life will happen, but it is our decision whether we get caught up in it, or whether we choose to follow Jesus and try to honour Him with all we think, say and do.

Daily Reading Plan Day 35: Numbers 3–4; Psalm 65.

Day 36: Blessed to be a Blessing

> *I will surely bless you and make your descendants as numerous as the stars in the sky and as the sand on the seashore. Your descendants will take possession of the cities of their enemies, and through your offspring all nations on earth will be blessed, because you have obeyed me." (Genesis 22:17–18)*

God made a covenant with Abraham, which included these verses from Genesis 22. God made it clear that He intended to give Abraham amazing blessings, and that as a result all the nations of the earth would be blessed.

God has provided enough resources for the whole world, but because so many of us do not grasp the vision from heaven's perspective, some people are rich and seem to get richer, while others are poor and seem to get poorer.

As we choose to put God's kingdom first, and see heaven as our treasure, it becomes our desire to see heaven's values established here on earth, which includes blessing the people we meet in our daily lives. And so, I ask the question, "As we live and interact with people, do we leave a trail of blessing or destruction behind us? Do we leave behind the aroma of Christ, or a bad smell?"

Sometimes we allow God to rule and reign in some areas of our lives, but others are locked, with a sign saying "GOD, KEEP OUT."

Ask the Holy Spirit to show you if you have any signs like that in areas of your life. Will you dare to give God complete authority? Will you submit totally to His will for your life, giving Him permission to guide you even more in the direction of being a blessing to everyone you meet.

When Jesus sent His disciples out, not everyone they met wanted to receive their blessing, and they were told to take the blessing back, and move on to someone else. It is the same for us. Not everyone will welcome the Holy Spirit inside us. But nevertheless, may it be our aim to bless others.

Daily Reading Plan Day 36: Numbers 5–6; Psalm 66.

Day 37: The Wilderness or The Promised Land

We will not receive any inheritance with them on the other side of the Jordan, because our inheritance has come to us on the east side of the Jordan." (Numbers 32:19)

Do you want God's best for your life, or are you prepared to settle for something less? Imagine that you are standing in the wilderness and you are offered 2 choices:

1. To go forward into the promised land which is flowing with milk and honey. There are still fierce battles to be fought in taking possession of the land, but it is ultimately the best place to live.

2. Or to stay where you are wandering in circles in the wilderness.

Will you go forward into God's promises or stay in the wilderness, where no faith is required? The Reubenites and Gadites decided that they wanted to live on the east side of the Jordan, rather than taking a further step into the promised land. In the wilderness there was some blessing. The land was fertile and they had prospered there to some degree, but it wasn't God's best for them. However, they weren't prepared to pay the price of taking hold of their inheritance on the West side of the Jordan. They chose the option with least risk and settled for second best.

Many Christians today make a similar choice. They may start out well, being happy to step out in faith and excited to see where God will take them next. But then later in life, they decide that they want to be more comfortable and settle into a compromise, instead of going for the promise.

There are also many who have never really stepped out in faith, to where they were totally dependent upon God for success. Perhaps no-one had modelled that way of life for them?

Either way, they have settled on the east side of their Jordan, and don't enter their promised land, where life is full of challenge and hope. Sure, there are battles to face, but with the sweet taste of victory in Christ.

Daily Reading Plan Day 37: Numbers 7–8; Psalm 67.

Day 38: Pursue Excellence

> *Then Jacob called for his sons and said: "Gather around so I can tell you what will happen to you in days to come. "Assemble and listen, sons of Jacob; listen to your father Israel. "Reuben, you are my firstborn, my might, the first sign of my strength, excelling in honour, excelling in power. Turbulent as the waters, you will no longer excel, for you went up onto your father's bed, onto my couch and defiled it. "Gad will be attacked by a band of raiders, but he will attack them at their heels (Genesis 49:1–4, 19)*

These are the words of Jacob to his sons Reuben and Gad, at the end of his life. With Reuben's and Gad's track records, Jacob knew that they were happy to just get by in life and wouldn't be interested in the effort it would take to take hold of God's best for them, and for their descendants. They could live the way they did without having to exercise any great faith in God. Life was comfortable.

We may at first think that their tribes settled east of Jordan because they had no heart to do battle to inherit the promised land. That is of course not true, they went ahead of the other tribes to fight together with them until the war was won. However, by remaining across the other side of Jordan they settled in God's second best for them. Spending time in the wilderness was intended to prepare them to cross the Jordan. But they weren't interested in God's plan for their lives. However, Jacob's other sons and their descendants chose to make the journey, and after many battles received God's best for their families.

Some people are willing to pay the price to receive God's best, and persevere, but others are not.

What about you? Is second best good enough for you? After all, it could be a lot worse. Do you have an "it will do" mentality? Or are you prepared to put in the effort required to live on the west side of your Jordan?

What spiritual, or natural, inheritance are we storing up for the generations who follow us?

Daily Reading Plan Day 38: Numbers 9–10; Psalm 68.

Day 39: Enter YOUR Promised Land!

Whoever does not take up their cross and follow me is not worthy of me. Whoever finds their life will lose it, and whoever loses their life for my sake will find it. (Matthew 10:38–39)

Jesus says that we only really find our life as we lose it and serve the purposes of his kingdom. Jesus presented a radical gospel, but it works!

God gave me a life-changing dream which I shall attempt to recount briefly:

He showed me that all the things in my life including my home, work and pension etc., which give a sense of security, are only an illusion. In my dream I met a man who asked me to give up absolutely everything which feels safe, and to travel with him, allowing him to feed me. I didn't know whether he was offering me just one meal, or whether there would be more. There was no offer of employment, and no other benefits. I was being invited to swap a comfortable life (with some struggles), for a life with a man who appears safe and secure, but having no idea where it will lead me?

In this earthly life, I think I know how things will work. Finances can be a struggle at times, but I am used to that. I have friends and family and life is reasonably good. If I follow this man, I have no idea where he will ask me to live and what he will ask me to do. But he will pay the bills. That's his part of the deal. Why am I hesitating? No more financial stress!

He asks me to trade my life, some of it good and some of it bad, for a life free of financial responsibility. It will be up to me to steward the resources he gives me to look after and use. But the buck stops with him and not me. He asks me to cast out my net on the other side of the boat where he is Lord. It's scary, but what a wonderful opportunity!

Jesus said, "Whoever would save his life will lose it, but whoever loses his life for my sake, will find it."

Will I do it? Will you do it?

That unknown territory is the promised land, our inheritance in Christ.

Daily Reading Plan Day 39: Numbers 11–12; Psalm 69.

Day 40: Enter YOUR Promised Land!

Whoever does not take up their cross and follow me is not worthy of me. Whoever finds their life will lose it, and whoever loses their life for my sake will find it. (Matthew 10:38–39)

Since our promised land is our inheritance in Christ, it is the place we follow him into. We may have many battles to face, but it is great to know our future is secure.

We may have accepted Jesus as Lord of our lives, but in reality not given him our whole life. There can be areas of our life which are kept firmly locked from him. This may be intentional, or we may be unaware of it.

Yet, it is my aim to hand everything over to him. It is what I am choosing to do because I know that I can't out-give God. I can give him all my rubbish and still receive blessings in return.

But what about the successes? Will I give Jesus these, too? When we have had success, we tend to think that they are our achievements, and we want to take the credit. We forget that we can only be successful by his grace. All our righteousness is as filthy rags!

Choose to repent of pride and put on Jesus's robe of righteousness. I'm sure the colour will suit you! Pure, white, spotless. Just like Jesus. You don't deserve to wear it, and nor do I. But we wear it by faith in Jesus, who is the author and perfecter of our faith.

I encourage you to exchange all you have for your inheritance in Christ, your promised land. It may not be an easy life, but Christ will give the victory, though not necessarily in the way you expect.

You will be greatly rewarded for living your life for the kingdom of God — some of it in this life and some in the next!

Daily Reading Plan Day 40: Numbers 13–14; Psalm 70.

www.ingramcontent.com/pod-product-compliance
Lightning Source LLC
Chambersburg PA
CBHW061310040426
42444CB00010B/2580